I Spy...Isle Royale

Susanna Ausema

As the boat pulls up to the great big dock,
I look all around and begin to take stock.
I promise I will tell you, or at least I will try,
to describe to you—all the wonders that I spy.

Isle Royale Queen IV

Voyageur II

Sea Hunter III

Visitors can travel to Isle Royale on one of four ferries, by private boat, or by seaplane. The ferry rides take up to six hours! Does it make you wonder how animals made their way to this isolated island?

I spy a squirrel with a fluffy red tail.

He jumped from a tree and ran down the trail.

Stashing seeds and mushrooms in his chubby little cheeks,

A special secret hiding place is surely what he seeks.

How did red squirrels make their way to Isle Royale? Perhaps by floating on a log, or by stowing away in a boat. Island researchers don't know for sure. For many years, researchers thought that the geographic separation over time had allowed the squirrels to evolve into a different subspecies from mainland squirrels. Recent DNA testing shows, however, that there's no genetic difference between them. We're continually learning more about Isle Royale's animals through the scientific studies being performed!

I spy a moose, munching on a tree,
So much food available—it looks that way to me.
Aquatic plants, leaves, twigs—they eat all this and more;
During summer food is everywhere, but winter choice is poor.

Moose are most active at dawn and at dusk. They are good swimmers; in fact, researchers think
that they originally arrived on Isle Royale by swimming from the North Shore of Lake Superior!
Moose are herbivores, which means they eat plants like the ones shown here. Every year, the
male moose grow antlers, which sometimes reach more than five feet wide.

I spy a wolf track in the middle of the trail.

The wolves are so elusive I've not even seen a tail.

I know they search for prey, and sometimes like to prowl;

Their location is well hidden—until they start to howl.

Wolves first arrived on Isle Royale in the late 1940s. They walked across an ice bridge from the North Shore of Lake Superior. Finding abundant prey in the form of moose, their population grew and the pack divided and spread out across the island in the following years. Eventually, the wolf population began to decline. Ask a ranger for up-to-date information about the wolves and moose on Isle Royale.

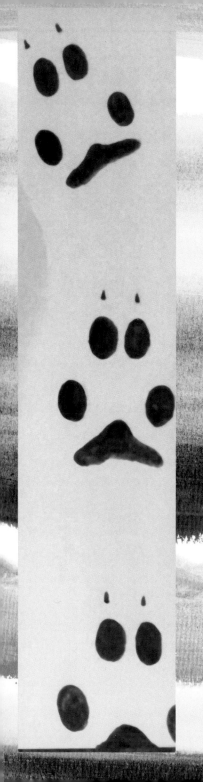

I spy a snowshoe hare, hiding in the grasses.
Its fur blends in, so the hungry fox just passes.
The fox trots away, following a smell;
Of its clever hiding place, the hare will never tell.

On Isle Royale, wolves and red foxes hunt snowshoe hares, so being camouflaged is important for the hares' survival. During the warmer months, their fur is brownish gray, but in the winter, it turns white to blend in with the snow.

I spy a dragonfly flitting through the air.

At first I saw just one, but now I see a pair.

I consider them among my friends because of what they eat:

They seem to think that 'skeeters are a very tasty treat!

Dragonflies can eat hundreds of mosquitoes in a single day. They have sharp teeth, but they actually catch insects with their feet. Each year, dragonflies in their larval stage are collected from four of Isle Royale's inland lakes. By measuring methylmercury contamination in dragonfly larvae, we can learn about contamination throughout the aquatic food web.

I spy a bird,
Flitting through the trees;
A white-throated sparrow
Or a black-capped chickadee.

Isle Royale is home to over 250 species of birds. The tiny
songbirds can be difficult to photograph or even see, but
they're easy to hear as they sing in a joyful harmony.

From boreal forests of fir and spruce
Inhabited by fox and moose,
To inland lakes full of pike and perch
Bordered by forests of aspen and birch,

I will continue to search and observe and share the things that I SPY!

I spy a pitcher plant in a squishy bog:
Its colors are quite beautiful, even through the fog.
There's something about the plant that surely tempts the flies—
Until they're swallowed up and eaten, taken by surprise!

Isle Royale is home to several species of insectivorous plants. Besides the
pitcher plant, there are round-leaved sundew and butterwort. If you're
hoping to see one, look in bogs and swamps. Just remember, you might run
into a lot of biting insects in these moist and humid places!

I spy a rock, orange and black and green.
These are not the colors of other rocks I've seen.
Something's growing on there, I notice while I'm hikin',
I know it's not a plant—it must be a lichen!

Most lichens are formed by a fungus and an alga growing together as one organism. (Some have a third partner—a yeast!) The fungus protects the alga from direct sunlight, absorbs water, and provides structure and an attachment point for the lichen. The alga, in turn, provides food for the fungus through photosynthesis. Lichens have the unique ability to grow on bare rock, which allowed them to colonize Isle Royale before other organisms. The lichens here may be hundreds of years old. With 600 species, Isle Royale is among the national park record holders for lichen diversity! Their presence is an indicator of good air quality.

I spy whitecaps, crashing on the shore.
They must be nearly five feet tall, maybe even more.
Planning on canoeing? You should change your mind.
Otherwise—most likely—you'll end up in a bind.

Lake Superior is the largest body of fresh water on Earth by surface area. Its average depth is 483 feet, and the maximum depth is 1,332 feet. Due to varying depth and weather conditions, Lake Superior can create waves large enough to sink freighters like the *Edmund Fitzgerald*. But on a calm day, exploring the island's inland lakes or Lake Superior shorelines can be very fun! If you're quiet, you never know what kind of wildlife you might happen upon: loons, moose, beavers, otters—or something else!

Lake Superior surrounds this island chain,

Where weather can be fierce, be it snow or rain.

The lake makes its weather and changes its mood,

And that can result in deep solitude.

I will continue to search and observe and share the things that I SPY!

I spy a fish in a clear, deep pool.

It shimmers when it swims, like a pretty little jewel.

Pink and gold with silver flashing underneath,

The colors are so vibrant, like an autumn-colored leaf.

Isle Royale has been a favorite fishing spot for centuries, first among Native American tribes, then commercial fishermen. Nowadays, visitors enjoy recreational fishing in the inland lakes, where they catch northern pike, walleye, and yellow perch, or in Lake Superior, where the fish are much bigger; lake trout up to 45 pounds have been caught! There are over 40 species of fish living within Isle Royale's waters.

I spy a frog, jumping through the grass.
Suddenly it stops, as if to let me pass.
"Ribbit, ribbit, ribbit," says the frog to the clouds,
At first very quiet, it becomes very loud.

Isle Royale is home to ten species of amphibians, although few are frequently spotted. The recognizable songs of some of the frogs might be the only indication of their presence. Wood frogs begin singing in the spring, followed by the loud chorus of spring peepers in early summer. Green frogs (shown here) and mink frogs are typically the last species singing in mid-summer. It's fun to look for tadpoles in the splash pools along the rocky shoreline of Lake Superior.

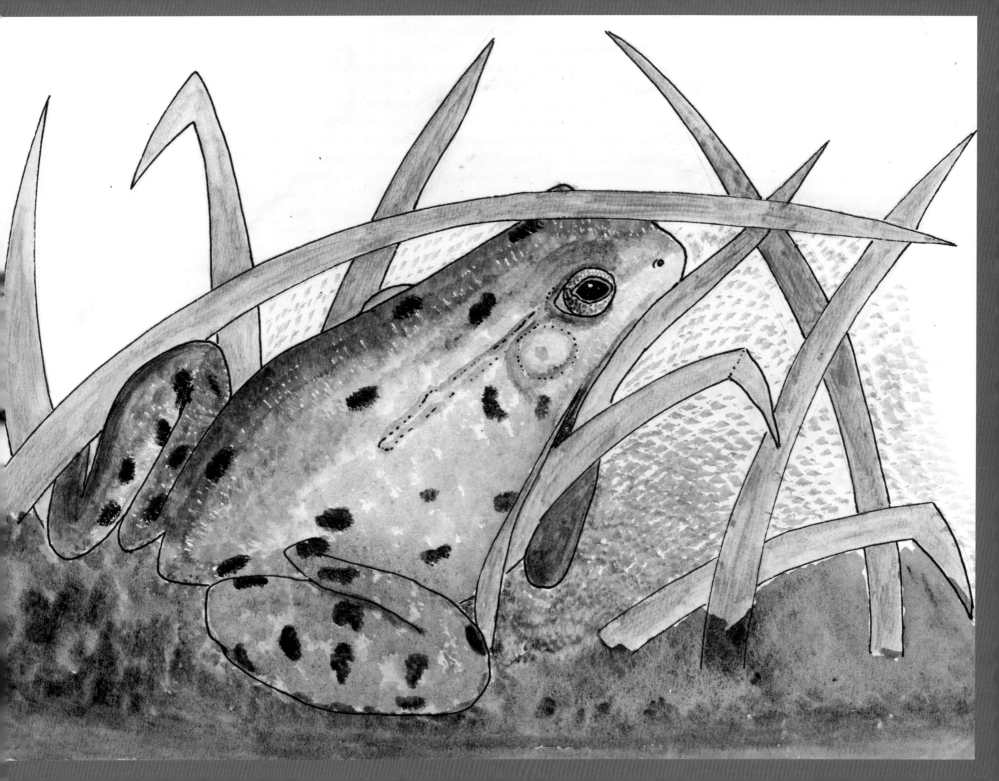

I spy a berry, small and round and blue;
I know that it is edible, so I eat a few.
Of the many berries that grow on this isle,
Blueberries are my favorite, so I gather a big pile.

Picking blueberries on Isle Royale has been a favorite activity of mine since
I was a small child. Some of my son's first island memories will probably
be hiking up to the Greenstone Ridge and picking berries for the rest of
the afternoon. The first berries begin to ripen in the middle of July, and
for the next couple of months, they become a staple in the diet of island
backpackers. Other delicious berries that grow abundantly on Isle Royale
are thimbleberries and raspberries. Island animals love the berries, too!

I spy a bird, its feathers white and black.

It dove under the water, but look—now it's back.

A haunting call rings out, and under the full moon,

The bird appears again and I know it is a loon.

The call of the loon is one of the most memorable sounds for many of Isle Royale's visitors. Loons successfully nest in many of the island's bays, harbors, and inland lakes. They communicate many things through their range of calls. One to pay extra attention to is the "tremolo," which can sound like crazy laughter but indicates that the loon feels threatened, possibly because you are too close.

I spy a boat waiting at the dock.

I know it's time to leave as I glance up at the clock.

This place is filled with beauty, excitement all around—

That's why I wrote this book for you, to show you what I've found!

Wolf

Muskrat

Moose

"Clues" left behind by wildlife on Isle Royale

Otter

Beaver

Fox

Jasper Ausema holds up a small moose antler on Isle Royale.

Moose

Wolf

Susanna Ausema spent her childhood summers on Isle Royale. Her father was a park ranger, and her mother was a park volunteer for many years. After moving away in her teens, she returned to work at Isle Royale as a seasonal ranger during her college years. There she met her husband, Mike, also a ranger, in 1998. Susanna continued her career as a permanent park ranger focusing on educational outreach at Curecanti National Recreation Area, Black Canyon of the Gunnison National Park, and Redwood National Park.

When her son, Jasper, was born, Susanna became a stay-at-home mom. When Jasper was two years old, the family moved back to Isle Royale and he began to explore the park as if it were his big backyard. Jasper loves books and Susanna loves to write, so she felt inspired to write a story for him about Isle Royale. After the text was complete, she looked around her pool of talented friends for someone who could illustrate it. None had the time to take on the (pro bono!) project, so Susanna picked up a paintbrush and started experimenting with watercolors. Jasper has helped her judge which styles and techniques are most interesting to a young audience, and together, they've put together this book.

Susanna's husband is the East District Ranger on Isle Royale, so they spend their days exploring and adventuring on Isle Royale during the summer and reveling in the autumn colors and abundant snow in the Keweenaw Peninsula during the rest of the year.

Susanna resumed her work on behalf of national parks in 2015 as the membership outreach manager for the nonprofit Isle Royale & Keweenaw Parks Association.

For my beloved son, Jasper

Design: Susanna Ausema
Digital Layout: Mike Stockwell, Cranking Graphics
Project Management: Kristine Bradof
Manufacturing: MidStates Printing

The Isle Royale & Keweenaw Parks Association is the member-supported, nonprofit cooperating association that partners with Isle Royale National Park and Keweenaw National Historical Park. IRKPA publishes educational materials about our parks and provides financial support for the parks' educational, historical, interpretive, and scientific missions.

For more information or to become a member, visit www.irkpa.org.

Isle Royale & Keweenaw Parks Association

All photos taken by Mike and Susanna Ausema, with the following exceptions:

Cover background photo—Carl TerHaar
Pg 2—*Sea Hunter III* by Charles Gerth
Pg 38—wolf track & otter scat, National Park Service photos
Pg 39—wolf scat by Katie Keller